THE CLOUD

OIL

Included

S. E. McKenzie

S. E. MCKENZIE

ISBN: 978-1-928069-27-0

ISBN- 1928069274

CLOUD: Oil included

DEDICATION
To everyone who has been left out in the cold.

S. E. MCKENZIE

This book is a book of speculative fiction. Characters, companies, governments, places, events, are either products of the author's imagination or used fictitiously. Any resemblance to persons (living or dead), companies, governments, places and/or events, is a coincidence.

CLOUD: Oil included

TABLE OF CONTENTS

S. E. MCKENZIE

CLOUD

S. E. MCKENZIE

CLOUD
I

There was a man called Dick
Who lived in a town that was toxic
Dick always felt sick

As he waited for the news
That was sad and gloomy
Wondering who he knew had been bruised

Dick was looking for a better way
But he never had a say
He hid from the vampires that drew blood

After they threw
Their neighbors' name
In the mud

There was no hello
All eyes were down
For Dick lived in a toxic town

CLOUD: Oil included

II

Dick was always told
That he would soon grow old
So he needed to find the path in a hurry

That was made of gold.
And Dick always did what he was told
So he kept his head in the cloud

For that was the only way
He would not feel lost in the crowd
That was the only way

He would know what was allowed
He signed up for service at eighteen
He already knew that the world was cold and mean

When he was in the cloud
Dick felt like a movie star
He felt that he would go far

S. E. MCKENZIE

Dick wanted his life to last.
The years went by a little too fast
He saved his past

In the cloud
Some of the memory faded away
Some of it would always stay

III
The cloud was alive
Twenty four hours a day
And a girl called Jill

Found it quite a thrill
She too felt like a movie star
She was told that she would go far

So she didn't think twice

When her life became an open book
She would walk down the streets of ice
And get a dirty look

CLOUD: Oil included

That was the price for individuality
That was the price for feeling free
The cloud was alive

For the cloud was powered by a super battery

IV
As the cloud ruled
It reigned from above
Data yours and mine

Flew in and out in time
At times it became lost
And crumbled in corruption

Dick could only whisper in frustration
When such loss
Caused cosmic interruption

"Where is my life?
It has been lost
This service was never meant

To have such a high opportunity cost."
The pages from years gone by
Were lost forever in the cloud

S. E. MCKENZIE

There was no fear
No human was near
And the super battery kept the cloud alive

As Dick fell to the ground
Dick was lost in a crowd
Dick couldn't speak too loud

Dick had no say
Dick had his pay
The money was stored in the cloud

Page by page
Dick's life faded away
Page by page

Dick had no say
In the process
That was run from a place across the sea

Day by day

CLOUD: Oil included

Though the cloud was stored
In that place so far away
The cloud's door could never be ignored

For the door to the cloud was in Dick's room
Where he looked for news
About gloom and doom

How could following such a path and direction
Not shape Dick's destiny
And fate's selection

They called him a bum
He lived in a slum
They said he was dumb

They left their garbage there
Cause no one would care
No one would dare

S. E. MCKENZIE

Oh do you see the pretty lights over there
Another street
That is watched closely

Another street
That the lowly
Are not welcomed or belong

As Dick fell from the cloud
And onto the ground
People came from all around

Some kicked him
Until he started to bleed
And all the good men

Did nothing at all
They just watched Dick crawl
He did not belong there at all

CLOUD: Oil included

V

As Dick crawled home
He was just barely alive
Living in a toxic town

You do what you do to survive
Dick opened the door to the cloud
And then made a cup of tea

He hoped that he would heal
From his wounds
So no one could see

How he was degraded
And humiliated
By those on the other side of the street

Who had better things to eat
Better shoes on their feet
It was hard not to feel defeat

S. E. MCKENZIE

Toxic town
People wearing a frown
Throwing all their garbage around

On Dick's side of the street
The red line could
Only be crossed carefully

Or you would get run down
By those in a rush
To get to the finer part of town

Now Dick was always aware
When you came tumbling down from the cloud
He wondered if he would ever be free

From all the negativity and toxicity
That was thrown all around
And kept Dick down

CLOUD: Oil included

In his toxic town
Where he always felt sick
Kept him in his place

The anger it swelled
And trapped him in misunderstanding
And labels so condescending

The anger it grew
And it made them laugh
As the joke grew crueler

Hate became the ruler
The thought police they were walking by
And looked at Dick in the eye

"What were you thinking?
When you crossed that street
You know they don't want you there

You know they will never care
So why were you waiting
For this world to grow more love

S. E. MCKENZIE

You must be soft in the head
If you wait too long
You will be dead"

VI

The cloud was as soft
As air
And it felt so safe up there

And Dick wanted independence
And to be free to be
Who he wanted to be

Dick had dreams
That were not in compliance
Some said they were an act of defiance

The thought police were everywhere
Some just stood there
Wearing a stare

For the next war would be in the air
It would feel safe
So many would not care

CLOUD: Oil included

There was talk of cyber war
Espionage
And sabotage

Even though
Dick was just hoping for love
He knew true love could only be

In a land that was free

VII

The threat was real
And lurked from the cloud
Could be disruptive and was not allowed

This cyber war was misunderstood
While power was everything in a city
Without lights things did not look as pretty

Without power and electricity
People would grow cold
Some would freeze to death

S. E. MCKENZIE

Before they grew old
Then the journey
To find the path

Which led to gold
Would be put on hold
And no one would be told

The cyber war
Was classified
So no truth could be spoken

Even though
Many knew
What they were fighting for

Even though inequality was denied
All that was allowed
In the cloud

Was deceit
To avoid defeat
And the thought police

CLOUD: Oil included

Were everywhere
In case someone thought otherwise
They would have to learn to despise

While looking into the enemy's eyes
For all was not what it seemed to be
This was now World War Three

Dick was not free and felt his captivity
Deep in his heart
This feeling tore him apart

He wanted to be free and independent
But he was told to hold the line
And be compliant

Otherwise
He would appear
To be defiant

And they would look right into Dick's eyes
And criticize
He was told the line to memorize

S. E. MCKENZIE

For it was now World War three
All around
There were feet stomping on the ground

VIII

During this war Dick had to be courageous
He was being watched
For any defiance could become contagious

The usual roar of war
Could not be heard
So this war was easier to ignore

Until the cloud came tumbling down
Broke into pieces
All around

Knowledge that had been passed down
Throughout the ages
Had to be saved somehow

Or there would be culture shock
One could lose the sense of time
Without a clock

CLOUD: Oil included

How could opportunity knock
If there was no door
Anymore

To the cloud
Where only silence was allowed
For secrets must be hidden from the crowd

Possessiveness could be an evil trait
And could lead to more
Conflict, war and hate

It was hard
Not to fight for possessions
When most of them were gone

What was left
Felt more precious
Easier to become more reckless

S. E. MCKENZIE

IX

The rule made it all one way
With no innovation or integration
How could there not be segregation?

The rule made it all one way
While the gap grew between
The east side and the west side

The door to the cloud
Was the only escape
Dick was allowed

For one must never speak
Or one would
Be disturbing the crowd

Privacy and identity
Went up in smoke
It was World War Three

In conditions of invisibility
Who was the enemy?
We just had to wait and see

CLOUD: Oil included

X

Dick dreamt of a day
When love and peace would be restored
The more he dreamt the more he was ignored

Even though Jill felt the same way
She knew that Dick
Was being watched everyday

Jill knew that Dick could never be free
So how could love ever be
The fate of tomorrow

Was shaped by the war in the air
It could not be seen
And therefore easy to ignore

Until the cloud came
Tumbling down
And fell into pieces all around.

THE END

S. E. MCKENZIE

OIL

CLOUD: Oil included

OIL

I

This tale is sad
But never intended
Peggy Lee and Stu

Had a garden which was unattended
As weeds grew out of control
A man knocked on their door

He showed Stu a map that was never shown before
Of many oil wells that were planned
He told Stu oil would always be in demand

For ever and ever
Which is always here
When you are rich

You have less to fear

S. E. MCKENZIE

II
The big machines
Toil for oil
Surrounding the earth in gooey spoil

The price of oil
Goes up and down
Controls the rate

Of currency
As price intertwines
With Peggy Lee and Stu's fate

Stu was told that the rich
Live better than most
Even though they may be haunted

By yesterday's ghost

CLOUD: Oil included

III

The rule of tiny bacteria
From years gone by
Cooked under pressure

In a patch underground
Liquid catch
If all goes well

Will gush from the ground
And into the bank almost owned by the Cartel
For ever and ever

Or so it seems
As Stu watched in awe
As his cash flow returned in endless streams

That oil stream over there
Drowned Peggy Lee's dream
Her fear was awoken

Once Stu's promise was broken

S. E. MCKENZIE

IV
Black Gold
Under your feet
Black gold cooks what you eat

Black gold gushed into the air
Even though birds
Were flying up there

Black Gold could change everything
For a while
Could even make Stu smile

As he packed his bags
He was gone
To a land where money could buy everything

Except true love
That he had
Forgotten

CLOUD: Oil included

V

Just another riddle
Ruled by supply and demand
Sometimes controlled

Sometimes in full swing
Fuels the engines of free enterprise
So loud

You won't hear the cries
Of the mother and her unborn
The steam hides the scream

Generated from a newborn's pure heart
When so many are torn apart
Peggy Lee clings to the past

As the future grew
Into a state unknown
Birds were trapped in gooey goo

S. E. MCKENZIE

Tankers protected by flags
Waving in the wind
High to low pressure

Big machines dig for treasure
As they dream for black gold and pleasure
Until these young men grow old

Boom town
Brown ground
The dream gushes into thin air

Supply spirals but still in control
Crude pegged into a rabbit hole
As a man called Stu

Left all his eggs in one basket

CLOUD: Oil included

VI

There will be a day
When prices climb to the sky
And then fall into the rabbit's dark hole

Volatile commodity without a soul
Finds a way to shrink
When all is wrapped up in black ink

Across the red line
The conflict can't be defined
No one knows what is wrong or right

Big rigs waving the flag all through the night
The red line defined
What was yours and what was mine

It was like the song
No one needed to sing along
For the music was designed to be listened to

When you were all alone

S. E. MCKENZIE

VII

That oil stream over there
Flowing through the pipe
Under the ground and waters too

Just another wild cat in the backyard
Owned by Stu
Became overnight millionaire

Always wanted to live like a sheik
As the oil gushed into thin air
It was black and it was sleek

His dream grew into what was true
Something that he could live by
Day by day

Such wealth gave Stu a new rank
And life too
He forgot that true love

Once kept him warm all night

CLOUD: Oil included

VIII

That oil stream over there
Drowned Peggy Lee's dream
Her fear was awoken once

Stu's promise was broken

Her heart sank into the abyss
When Stu found wealth that came gushing out
Like a fountain with no cup to hold

The overflow

All of that black gold; so he left her
Broken hearted
As he departed

Stu had a new life now
For he had become a backyard millionaire
Almost overnight

Even though Peggy Lee's love
Had kept him warm all night
For many years gone by

S. E. MCKENZIE

IX

As oil fueled the economic engine
The demand for oil was never done
As the flags waved silently through the night

They were still waving under the morning sun
The newborn with heart so pure
Was dammed to fate

That black gold
Would dictate
As the war of words was being spun

The newborn's war had just begun
His life that was already on the line
Before he could walk or talk

He was given a toy gun
As the years went by
He learned to run

At the beginning it was so much fun

CLOUD: Oil included

X

Love was a joy
Kept one motivated and fit
Kept one wanting more

As we toiled for oil
Oil gave us the steam
To fight for the American dream

Above ground
The pipes could not be seen
As oil was moved under the earth

It was clearly the supply stream
Everyone was hoping for
Would prevent war for land

That was clearly in demand
And was the very surface for feet
To walk upon

S. E. MCKENZIE

XI

The strategic goal was to foil
The opposition's
Quest for oil

And as the machines toiled for oil
The supply went up in flames
There were names
On the list to be blamed

As demand soared
Some called it an embargo
As the lines grew

As Peggy Lee saw the smoke
Took her bike
And rode away

Hoping to find a turn on the path
Of fate
Hoping to turn this hate

Around
Even if it meant
Keeping the oil in the ground

CLOUD: Oil included

XII

How can you not fear
The scorched earth policy
To win the oil war

The oil lakes
On fire
You see the mistakes

Made by the power that is screaming
While the new born
Is scheduled to be

Newborn has no say
He is just so glad to be alive
And loved

Pure heart
Pure mind
In uniform by 2033

S. E. MCKENZIE

XIII
The spirit of oil
Was not free
How could it be?

The energy of fire
Gains like a liar
Short term

In the order of things
Oil is supplied
With all kinds of strings

Which become undone
Before the end
Some things when broken

Can never mend
With flexibility
Could learn to bend

CLOUD: Oil included

Spilled oil all over the place
The demand cannot change
Until the price fluctuates

One side has supply in cap
The other has demand and need
How far will they go

To satisfy the oil god
Watching us
Burning in greed

Can you say?
Or will you lose your head
Can you say?

Through all this fear
The machines toil
For more oil

After we are all dead

S. E. MCKENZIE

The year without summer
Felt so poor
Though signs of wealth were all around

Frost bit at leaves
And bit at fruit
As long as there was gas for the car

Few really gave a hoot
They turned on the heat
And used more oil

As the machines toiled
People stayed inside
So they never saw

What had been spoiled

CLOUD: Oil included

The sun's rays tried to shine
But the dust and smoke
Blocked its power

Peggy Lee wondered were Stu might be
She remembered how love
Kept them warm all night

During this year without summer
Peggy Lee hoped for Stu's return
Though she never heard from him again

She waited anyway
As her youth faded away
The flowers could not bloom

The frost had bitten them too soon

S. E. MCKENZIE

XIV

Oh can you see the cap on the well
It cannot stop the oil from gushing
Out in thin air

Can you see the machines toil for oil
They do it all day
They do it for no pay

They can't remember the time
When oil did not matter
When oil slept undisturbed

Without care or sense of time
Then one day the wild cat tempted Stu
And then the supply of oil it just grew

And some said that it was all a trap
Supply side to control demand to a degree
As price tumbled and fell

The scorched earth policy
Reigned
Until Earth became hell

THE END

CLOUD: Oil included

Produced by S.E. McKenzie Productions
First Print Edition January 2015

Enquiries: 1(778)992-2453
Mailing Address:
S. E. McKenzie Productions
168 B 5th St.
Courtenay, BC
V9N 1J4

Email Address:
messidartha@aol.com

www.ingramcontent.com/pod-product-compliance
Lightning Source LLC
Chambersburg PA
CBHW060544030426
42337CB00021B/4424